Publisher

Bravely Beautiful Books

Dance with your Journey

Inspirational poetry

Author and Editor

Betsy L Theodore

Jared M Oliver

EverythingGood Fine Art Photography

To my amazing family,

Thank you for your support over the years the gratitude of love from each of your hearts. To my gorgeous baby girl Vivian for motivating apart of my soul I never knew existed. To my Parents, Jacki my mother, thank you for saving me and giving me everything that you could. A life that I wouldn't have without you, John my father may you rest in peace you were my rock, my first love. Malinda (Mia) my other mother children are lucky if they have one but I was blessed with two, thank you for all the love you didn't have to give. Mark, thank you for everything you provided for me over the years..... my hero's. To my mother's for teaching me how to be a lady and raising me with such grace and being amazing role models. To my father's for teaching me to be strong and to never stop believing in myself. Thank you for saving my life, an incredible journey and heroism that isn't recognized enough. I am where I am today because of all of you. Thank you to my incredible sisters and brothers we all share the same heart. To my best friends for listening to a new poem and supporting me from the time we were young. I dedicate this to you... with all of the love a world can give, I give to you.

I love you

Betsy Lynn

Table Contents

Dance with your Journey

Memorizing your moments through life, seeking that thirst in each season.

Are we traveling in one Journey?

Fearing that temptation, that want, that will.

Being the witness of the truth of your travels.

Listening for that voice of vision, kneeling to your temple

and learning to dance with your Journey.

The understatement of an artist.

A true artist is never on time. The gratitude of the finished project,

is the reward.

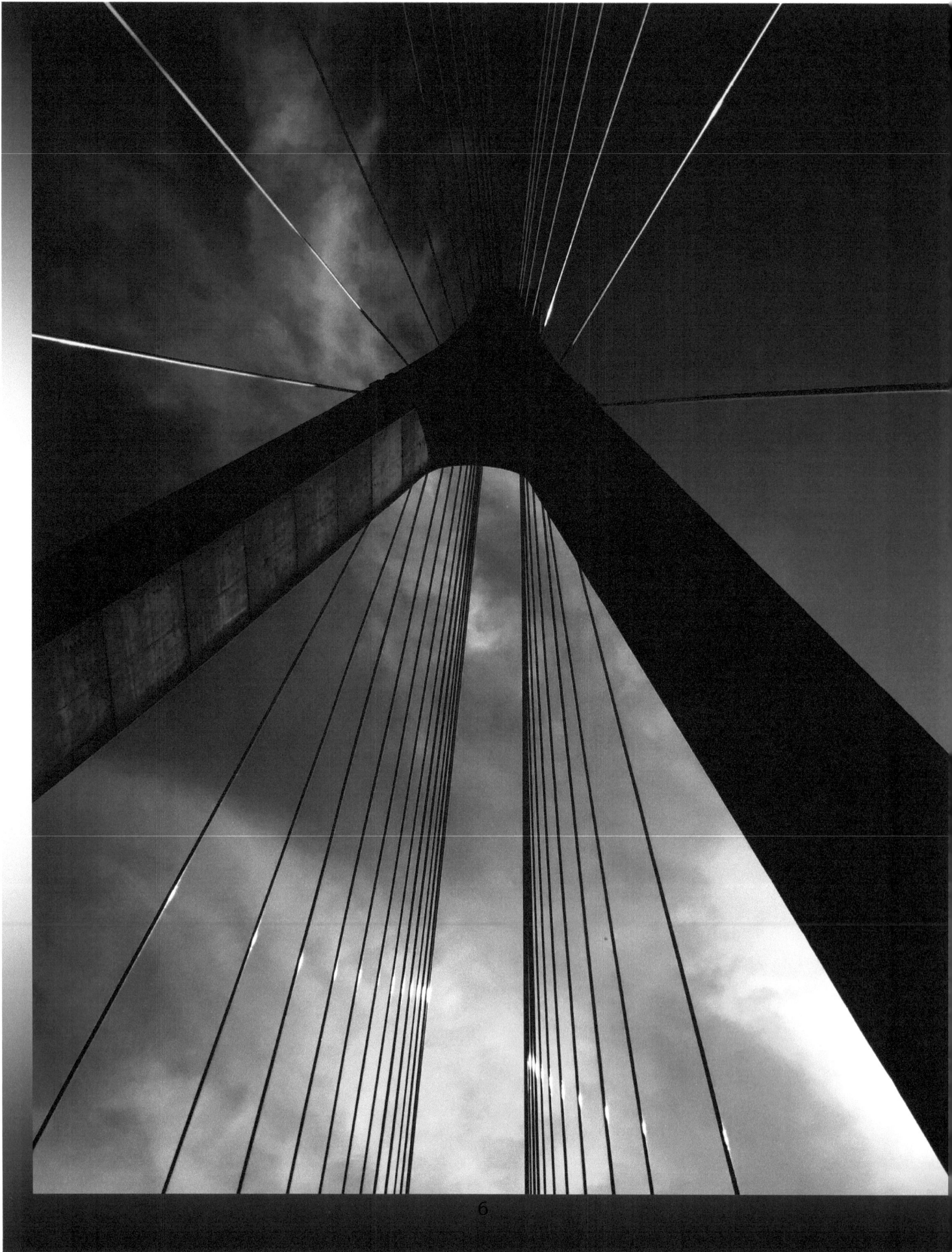

Writers

Is it that we speak of the same story but know how to write it within
a million different ways.

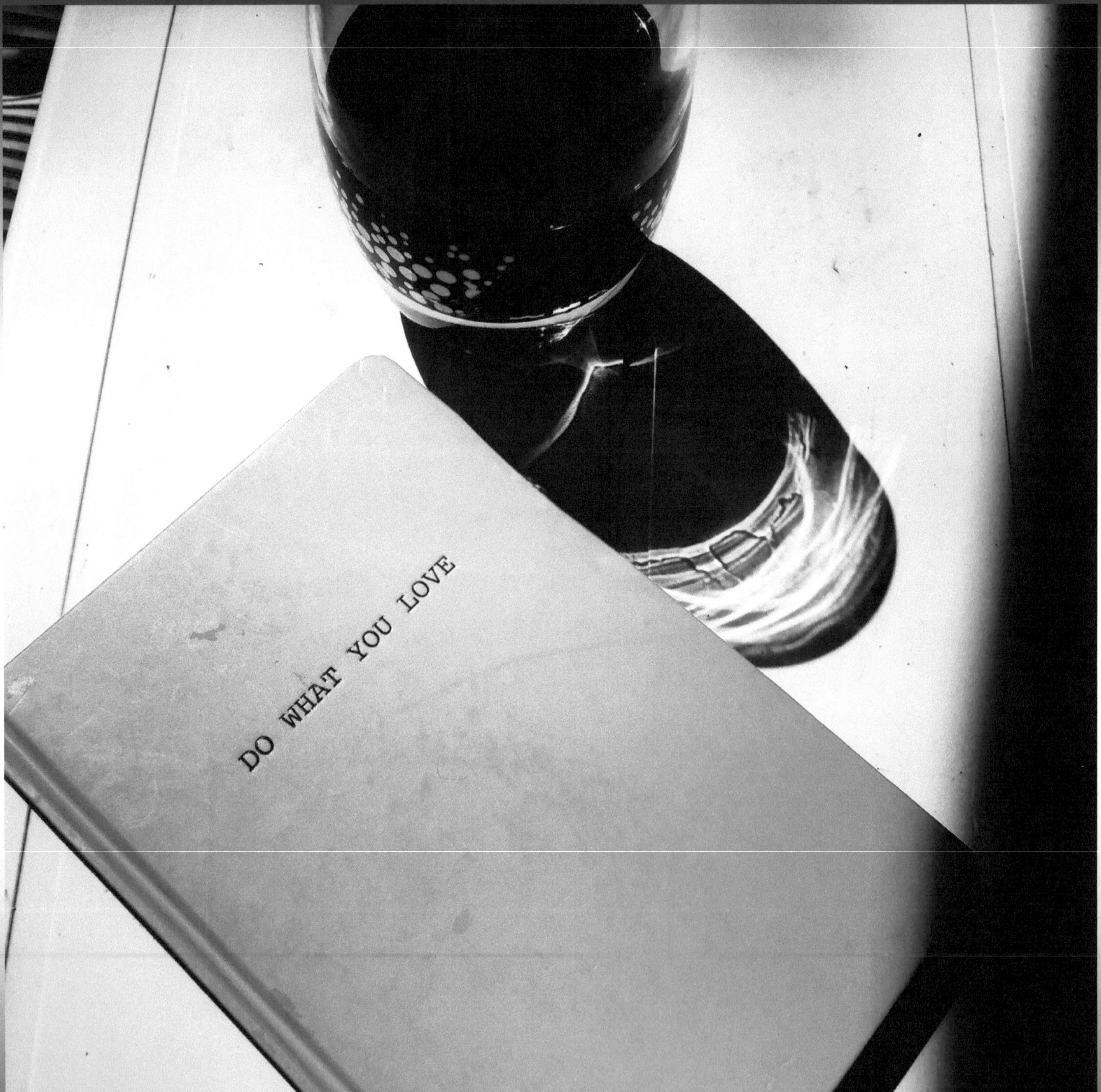
DO WHAT YOU LOVE

A writer's love is a lost soul's confessions.

Don't let it be a long road of worries you wish you hadn't wasted.

Every path is a lesson and every step is courage to see a better dream.

Weary Boots

So many thoughts in my heavy head though my heart feels scared but fulfilled. What do you think in the morning? What's your next step?

The boots lying in front of me...the long hours that they see, the sweat and fears of every step. The travels they go and at some point to weary beat up boot.

Is it like our life? Is it that we are scared to take that next step?

Is it that we have been abused to that very fine wrinkle beyond your eyes that defines your travels through life? The tears that have fallen or the smile that we share? Worries that you wish you hadn't wasted but we forget so easily. So quick to forgive but so easy not to forget, forgetting is what teaches us though. How do you embrace life with not being able to argue your simple thought or maybe your heart?

You want to forget why that situation made you feel so empowered to make a difference in the next. At the sunset of everyday isn't that why we are here? What are you here for? Here to hurt? Here to see? Here to feel? Here to love? Here to make a difference? At some point through your travels maybe in weary boots, know that you have made a difference in someone's life, as they have for you.

The person who I was, the person who I've become is the person I'm going to be.

An unapologetic sorry speaks volume of one's behavior.

May I cry today and may I rise tomorrow.

The fight

Isn't it funny how one simple moment can change your entire life?

The moment when you're not sure to go left or to go right? In these moments, do you celebrate the win? No you celebrate the overall conquer of the fight!

Some scars run deep, some fade and some heal in time...

In the end let it be an arrow and be true to your horizon.

Photograph

Candle light dancing on your reflection. A moment in time, a capture of your beautiful soul.

One more kiss, one more hug, one more I love you. Although the art you built was our foundation for years to come. The glass protects you from my tears the vision of so many years of love.

You are all around me I can see your reflection, I can feel your soul.

For now until we meet again I'll hold your photograph.

Ocean desire

The deep blue ocean desires the waves burning like fire.

Sand kicks up onto my legs as I reach for the waves. Have you ever seen such beauty? Life beholds waiting for me, the never ending water, so much out there but only blue my eyes can see.

It's almost as precious of a blooming rose,

the sensual water touching my toes.

The whispers of the wind carry within. It is a heaven shore, a

path to our fathers door.

Only blue my eyes can see life beholds waiting for me.

Sand kicking up onto my legs as I reach for the waves.

Waves untouchable burning like fire, as I stare at the deep blue ocean desire.

Soothe my soul by your love, strengthen my soul by your hate.

Inspire

Inspire me to change, to find a better me.

Inspire me to love, like it's the first time.

Inspire me to embrace each beautiful moment of life.

Inspire me to forgive, each enemy of their ignorance.

Inspire me to laugh, so hard that I cry.

Inspire me to teach, to let the fear go.

Inspire someone today, to change, to love, to embrace, to forgive, to laugh, to teach.

Inspire me the desire to dream

Don't let a jaded heart discolor yours.

My life is a beautiful note, in God's symphony.

Embrace

Have you ever heard a song without words? The most beautiful song is the one you write. Listening to a song without words all though it's the most beautiful piece because it's yours.

Don't give up, keep dreaming, love you and the life you are given.

Write your own notes, dance to your song and embrace each ending.

A photograph is capturing a piece of the soul in time.

Daddy's Voice

When you go through life and find yourself writing about it you are experienced, you have gained wisdom. To hear some speak and to teach is one simple lesson but when you understand their thoughts is when you have experienced the knowledge, you have gained.

To be able to speak and teach you have gained wisdom all though wisdom at some point will teach you not to speak only to listen.

To my best teacher... my father I was always listening

John Edward Theodore

1953—2014

I'm my father's daughter with my mothers touch.

Open your eyes

Life everything you ever wanted?

Do you ever question every point in your life?

Are you accomplished with family, love, career?

The moment when you realize you feel defeated.

That moment when you open your eyes to the truth.

You must do the right thing... let go.

Change with me like the leaves in autumn.

I'm a country girl with a New Yorker's ambition.

If you ever hurt someone it hurts you most, be beautiful to life.

Time

The clouds hush by hiding her pride. The cold promising breath that she keeps holding inside. The worn eyes taken by life. The lift of every crisp morning, she crawls to the mirror dragging her smile leaving her heart behind. What is she thinking? Though only a thought can never end, learning to be her best friend. The tears she cries and the laughter she brings, the hope she carries, the song she sings. How far is she going to go, where does it stop? She wants to laugh, laugh so loud! Slowly she brings upon herself a sweet tickling smile. Wondering if everything would be okay, no worries like a kiss from a peach, so soft and harmless.

Life awaits and she just smiles

Don't mistake my confidence for your insecurities.

50 Photo credit: Jared M Oliver

Be a bird and let your soul fly.

Keep your kisses

Let the sounds of the night swallow you with silence, opening your eyes as the warm orange glow of the sunset haunts your heart. Blinding what's in front of you. Falling in to the next chapter of character.

Be as brilliant as the Beatles,

colorless of a city,

brave as a warrior that's never been wounded.

Let the fear wash away with it's tide.

Love without limits and keep your kisses.

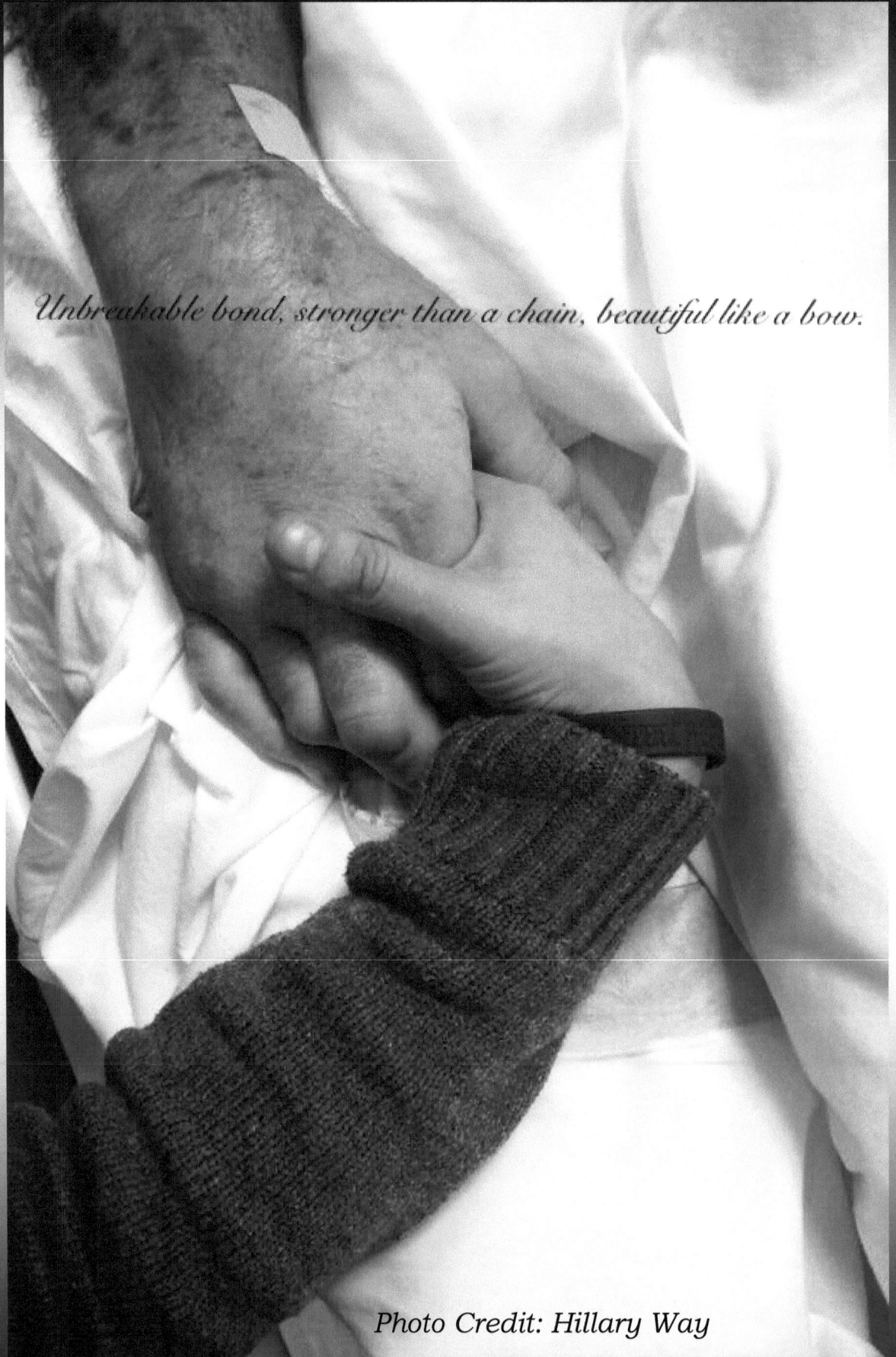

Unbreakable bond, stronger than a chain, beautiful like a bow.

Photo Credit: Hillary Way

They say it comes in waves, they say it will heal in time.

Reality is learning to live without you is an empty shore to my soul.

One in a million

Daddy did something to his daughters....

He instilled passion to drive a million hearts crazy.

A work ethic to make a million men look lazy and he gave us un-
conditional love to heal entire country.

Sometimes water is thicker than blood it just depends on the river God sends you on.

Photo credit Meghan Miller

He painted my wings and when he thought I was ready he taught my gypsy soul to fly.

An insecure woman is only lead by the most insecure man... A insecure man is an unattractive accessory to woman.

If you want them to listen wear red lips.

Let your heart rise above the noise and your success be heard with God.
Betsy L Theodore

Photo credit: Jared M Oliver

There's nothing more beautiful on a woman than confidence,
courage and red lips. Be brave, be beautiful.

Should you speak when ignorance arrives or let it fail your heart not knowing? Then God spoke to her as he laid a ray of angels upon her face.

God's Confidence

People may interpret confidence as many things in life. To me Confidence is being young and naïve or ignorant to your surroundings. Confidence is knowing every step of your journey and piecing the result. Closing your eyes as you vision it and sailing because you will conquer it. Confidence is walking into a room and knowing that they may stare out of admiration or hate. Confidence at some point will teach you to let the insecurities go, the doubt go, the hate go. One day you look in the mirror.... Confidence you finally see what God see's. Your inner beauty finally thrives on the outside.

There is nothing that can break you and nothing you can't overcome. By the grace of God he has instilled this passion of a thousand prayers and the strength of a thousand sins. The only forgiveness you have is with love and kindness. When you love all of you, you too will have gained God's Confidence.

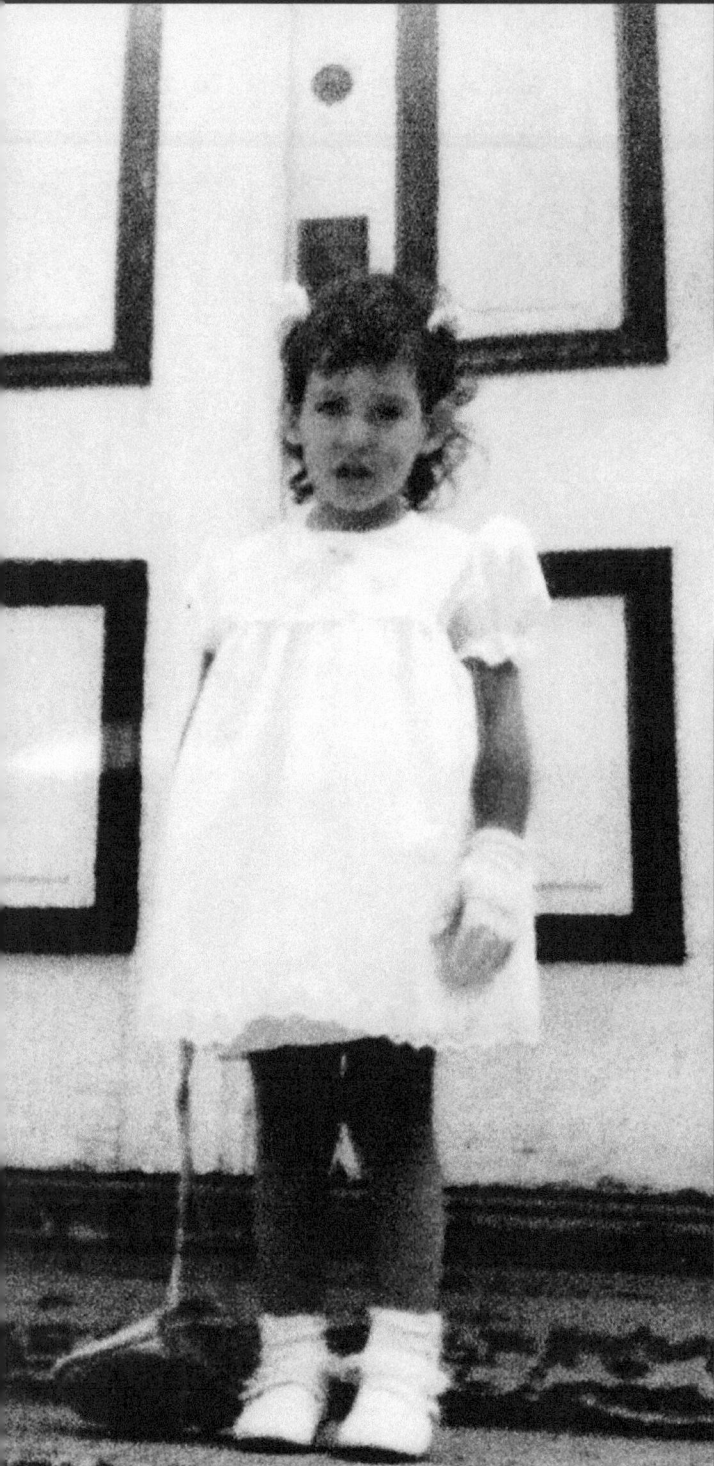

Photo Credit: Jared M Oliver

www.ingramcontent.com/pod-product-compliance
Lightning Source LLC
Chambersburg PA
CBHW041426090426
42741CB00002B/44